San Diego Wild Animal Park Habitats

ASIAN
WATERHOLE

MOUNTAIN
HABITAT

SOUTHERN
AFRICA

MONGOLIAN
STEPPE

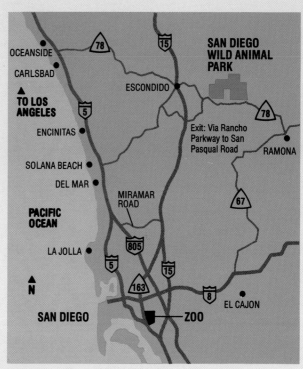

Location of the San Diego Wild Animal Park within San Diego County.

ISBN: 0-917859-08-1
Library of Congress No. 85-062253

Project Manager: Martha Baker
Design: Gay Hagen
Editing: Linda S. Davis
Maps: Ginny Brush
Production Art: Frank Becker
Coordination: Nicky Leach
Typesetting: Friedrich Typography
Printing: Frye & Smith

Produced by Sequoia Communications for
San Diego Wild Animal Park
15500 San Pasqual Valley Rd.
Escondido, CA 92027 - 9614

The San Diego WILD ANIMAL PARK

Text by Bill Bruns

Photographs by Ron Garrison and F. D. Schmidt

CONTENTS

Left: The Indian barasingha (Cervus d. duvaceli) *is an endangered deer native to northern India and southern Nepal. Full-grown stags often have 12 points to their antlers.*

Above: The Turkomen markhor (Capra falconeri heptneri) *is threatened in its native habitats of Russia and Afghanistan due to hunting for its impressive horns.*

Cover: Sumatran tiger (Panthera tigris sumatrae).

Previous page: Addra gazelles (Gazella dama ruficollis), *the largest members of the gazelle family, are true desert dwellers. They migrate north and south across the Sahara, according to the seasons.*

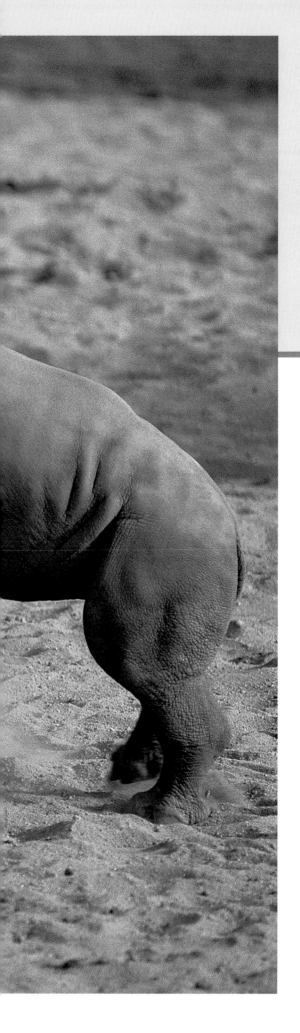

INTRODUCTION

Early in 1971, a prized shipment of endangered animals — 20 southern white rhinoceroses — left the port of Durban, South Africa, destined for their new home at the San Diego Wild Animal Park, sister facility of the world-famous San Diego Zoo. The white rhino had been rescued from virtual extinction by South African conservation efforts, and now surplus animals were being sent abroad in an effort to further safeguard the species' future. Only one white rhino had ever been born in captivity, but experts hoped the Wild Animal Park, with its spacious exhibits, could nourish a reproducing herd that would help populate other zoos worldwide.

After 25 treacherous days at sea and a journey by train and truck from Galveston, Texas, the rhinos were safely released into a 93-acre enclosure at their new home 30 miles northeast of San Diego. Yet the question remained: would the animals reproduce?

Since the new herd's males were sexually immature, a designated sire, Mandhla, was transferred — with trepidation — from the San Diego Zoo. In nine years there, he hadn't shown the slightest romantic interest in his female companion. However, when given open spaces and a large herd to stimulate his reproductive instincts, Mandhla sired 59 calves over the next 13 years, until he was shipped to another zoo to make room for a new male bloodline.

Thanks in part to Mandhla's efforts, and to continued breeding success in protected African reserves, the southern white rhino has been removed from the endangered species list. Moreover, the white rhino has come to symbolize the Wild Animal Park's vital role in worldwide efforts to protect and reproduce as many endangered species as possible — from elephants, gorillas, cheetahs, and lions to antelopes, deer, condors, and hornbills. The Park offers superb family entertainment and a unique opportunity to view a remarkable diversity of animals, but its primary purpose is to provide a naturalistic haven that helps ensure the survival of imperiled wildlife.

Commented Charles Bieler, executive director emeritus of the Zoological Society of San Diego, on the tenth anniversary of the Wild Animal Park in 1982, "Ongoing efforts here are essential if we are to provide an opportunity for our children and grandchildren to see many of the wonderful creatures that are dwindling in their native habitats and that soon may not be available ever again for viewing in the wild."

This guidebook will provide a clearer understanding of the dedicated attention given to the animals at the San Diego Wild Animal Park and the wide-ranging endeavors — by curators, veterinarians, keepers, researchers, horticulturists, and other staff — to nurture a self-sustaining collection of exotic animals that can benefit the San Diego Zoo and zoological institutions around the world.

When the San Diego Wild Animal Park was formally dedicated in bright, warm weather on May 9, 1972, its overall commitment was expressed in this official theme:

> *Join us here ... to contemplate the wild animals of the world and nature's wilderness ... to strengthen a commitment to wildlife conservation throughout the world, and to strive toward man's own survival through the preservation of nature.*

By devoting itself to this theme, the Wild Animal Park has matured into one of the most distinctive and successful wildlife preserves in the world. Spread across hills and valleys that are similar to biogeographic regions in Africa and Asia, the Park encompasses 1,800 acres, of which 700 have been developed into Nairobi Village, a lush 17-acre "port of entry," and naturalistic exhibits ranging up to 125 acres.

Nairobi Village is the visitor's first experience within the Wild Animal Park. At the entrance, you make a psychological break with the automobile environment by walking through a towering free-flight aviary filled with swirling, chattering tropical birds flitting about in a jungle setting of flowers, ponds, and bridges.

This 220-foot-long aviary leads into a bustling village with Africa-inspired structures offering food service, gift shops, a petting Kraal where visitors mingle with young animals being hand-raised in the Animal Care Center, and amphitheaters for staging the Wild Animal Park's famous animal shows.

Among the animal exhibits within Nairobi Village are Hanuman langurs, spider monkeys, ring-tailed lemurs, guenons, koalas, golden lion tamarins, slender-horned gazelles, and one of the few lowland gorilla families in captivity — all in enclosures set amid exotic flora and nearby waterfowl lagoons. Another walk-through aviary is Tropical America, in which deer, squirrel monkeys, and colorful birds roam freely in a rain forest habitat.

Two types of "safaris" lead out of Nairobi Village, affording distinctly different ways in which to see the Wild Animal Park's vast animal collection.

First, the Wgasa Bush Line monorail provides a five-mile, 50-minute journey past the main exhibits and smaller enclosures for such species as Grevy's zebra, Arabian oryx, Przewalski's wild horse, greater kudu, bongo, and okapi. As the electric-powered train silently glides by on rubber wheels, scenes right out of the wilds appear: herds of hoofed animals grazing peacefully on grassy hillsides, giraffes galloping off in their stately manner, impalas and springbok leaping into the air, wildebeests traveling together in large herds, babies running with their mothers, and animals in social groups challenging each other for territoriality. "It is without doubt one of the greatest shows in the zoo world," wrote Robert Bendiner in *The New York Times*.

Second, the 1.25-mile Kilimanjaro Trail offers a close-up of animals and plants viewed panoramically on the monorail journey. The trail initially wends through the Australian Rain Forest, where tall eucalyptus trees form a canopy of shade for resident animals — emus, kangaroos, wallabys, and many colorful Australian birds. Then, walk out to Pumzika Point, an observation platform from which residents in the Eastern Africa exhibit can be viewed. The trail then winds past landscaped enclosures housing ground hornbills, cheetahs, Sumatran tigers, Asian lions, African and Asian elephants, and lowland nyala.

Top: A herd of Indian axis deer or chital (Cervus a. axis) provides a spectacle of spots for passengers on the Wgasa Bush Line monorail as it travels past the Asian Plains. Summer evening tours showcase the animals' nocturnal behaviors.

Bottom: The Congo River Fishing Village, a landmark within Nairobi Village, replicates the catwalks over rapids and wooden fishing traps found in tribal communities throughout central Africa.

Following page: The Wild Animal Park leases 1,800 acres from the city of San Diego. The land is within the city's agricultural preserve in the San Pasqual Valley, where commercial development is restricted. Inset: In 1970, then Zoological Society Director Charles Schroeder planted stakes in the rugged hillsides, to plan the route for the Wgasa Bush Line monorail tour.

Birth of the San Diego Wild Animal Park

T he San Diego Wild Animal Park owes its existence to
Dr. Charles Schroeder, the far-sighted, persevering fellow
who became director of the San Diego Zoo in 1953. Even
then, one of his primary goals was to develop the Zoo's captive-
breeding capabilities to reduce its reliance on dwindling stocks
of animals in the wild. By 1959, he was convinced that a large
auxiliary facility was needed outside the city where the Zoo could
house surplus animals, breed larger species, and stock sizeable
breeding groups, whose offspring could be used to replenish the
Zoo or to trade with other zoos.

Not until 1962, however, did Schroeder's land search turn up
what he regarded as an ideal site: a dry, remote, 1,800-acre parcel
of San Diego city-owned land in the San Pasqual Valley. Then the
real challenge began, testing Schroeder's conviction that a
spacious, open-air animal reserve was an urgent necessity for the
Zoological Society of San Diego. Even his most ardent supporters
had difficulty visualizing great things for this sagebrush-covered
terrain, but Schroeder envisioned what the land could become
in time, and he conveyed that enthusiasm to key people on the
Society's board of trustees.

Schroeder's project was originally perceived as sort of a
"back-country zoo" with limited public participation — a simple
restroom, a snack bar, and perhaps an overview of some animals
— to be completed at a total cost of less than $1 million. Yet by the
time the board of trustees gave their go-ahead in 1969, Schroeder
felt the reserve could serve as a captive-breeding center and a
major source of public education regarding wildlife.

"We ended up spending $10 million by opening day,"
Schroeder recalled, laughing. "And today the place pulls
in more than a million visitors a year."

A final crucial hurdle was cleared in 1970, when San Diego
voters approved a $6-million private-bond proposal to provide
funding to build Nairobi Village and install the monorail system.   11

Just before opening day in 1972, Nairobi Village was little more than a few Africa-styled buildings. Today, the Village spans 17 acres and is a verdant jungle teeming with exhibits and activities.

With an ambitious Park concept now approved, Schroeder knew his staff would have to adapt the San Pasqual Valley landscape to the needs of exotic wildlife *and* the people desiring to see the wildlife without jeopardizing the sense of sanctuary that, for many animals, is essential to sustained breeding success. This eliminated, for example, a drive-through "safari park." Instead, after examining a variety of public transportation systems, the study committee wisely chose an electric monorail system that runs silently on rubber wheels and is nonpolluting.

Also expanding on the original concept, Wild Animal Park officials realized that close-up observation of some of the animals would attract visitors, perhaps making the Park a tourist attraction that eventually could become self-supporting. Thus, Nairobi Village and the Kilimanjaro Trail were created. Today, these areas are enveloped in luxuriant greenery — blanketed with more than a

million trees, including eucalyptus that tower 100 feet high.

Building the Animal Population

Meanwhile, in 1969, Jim Dolan, then associate curator of birds, began to accumulate the Wild Animal Park's animal collection. Dolan had come to the San Diego Zoo in 1963 from the Catskill Game Farm with master's and doctoral degrees in hoofstock management. In Schroeder's estimation, "He was the most capable guy we had for this job."

Faced with the unusual task of stocking a modern zoological park from scratch, Dolan transferred some animals from the San Diego Zoo and acquired the rest from other zoos, reserves, and animal dealers. Once they arrived, the animals were housed in holding pens

until the exhibits were completed.

"We concentrated heavily on acquiring hoofstock, especially endangered species, because the Park's terrain and climate are geared to that type of animal," said Dolan, who today is general curator of mammals for the Society. "We also designed exhibits that were large enough to allow for herds of up to 60 or 70 individuals of a gregarious species."

As Dolan wrote in ZOONOOZ®, the Society's monthly magazine, "The old zoo concepts for managing large animal species had to be put aside and new methods for their husbandry undertaken if long-term, self-sustaining populations were to be established as safeguards against extinction. Such a goal could not hope to achieve the necessary success where only two or three individuals of a given species could be accommodated. Genetic diversity would be greatly reduced, which could ultimately lead to the collapse of the entire project."

Dolan eventually had to determine the population mix inside the five main exhibits. His decisions were based primarily on the geographic region the animals came from in the wild and his own knowledge as to which species might peacefully coexist.

One unsuccessful experiment involved the Grevy's zebras. Starting out in Eastern Africa, the zebras were moved to their own hillside exhibit along the monorail route because they continually attacked young animals, especially baby wildebeests and impala.

Through daily observations, field keepers learned to sense which animals didn't fare well in close proximity to other species. The nyala, for example, are beautiful but solitary antelopes who hide their babies in rocky areas. They proved unsuited to their initial home in Southern Africa, and today have their own wooded hillside enclosure along the Kilimanjaro Trail.

Zoological Society goodwill ambassador Joan Embery was among the celebrities present on opening day, May 10, 1972. Elephant washes are still a favorite show for Wild Animal Park visitors.

13

Landscaping Challenges

One early physical adjustment (and a problem that still exists) was to make the Wild Animal Park predator-proof. Perimeter fencing controlled resident animals, except for rare escape attempts, but local predators such as coyotes persistently dug their way in through weak spots caused by rain and erosion, making off with newly born antelopes or gazelles. Anti-predator wire underneath the perimeter fence and greater surveillance of the fence line have substantially curbed the problem.

Wild Animal Park officials realized other growing pains as some early concepts proved unrealistic. "Originally, landscaping the main exhibits wasn't given much importance," recalled Jim Gibbons, manager of horticulture. "The philosophy was, 'Just turn the animals loose.' There was plenty of native ground-cover and vegetation out here, and since we were feeding the animals, they would never bother it. But many of these animals were browsers and they ate or trampled the thickets of brush that covered the hillsides. The place was bare within two years. Since the soil (decomposed granite) erodes easily, we realized that, if the Park was going to survive, we had to do something to stabilize the hillsides and valleys."

Erosion was not only depositing unwanted silt into small lakes in the Eastern Africa and Southern Africa exhibits, but also created dangerous ditches and gullies for the animals, and could eventually undermine the monorail tracks.

To keep the soil in place, while providing a supplementary food supply for certain species, the Wild Animal Park installed an extensive irrigation system in the field exhibits and hydroseeded large areas with grass. "We tried different groundcovers," said Gibbons, "but grass is the only thing we've found that will grow faster than the animals can eat it."

This continual "greening" of the Wild Animal Park is expensive — about $5,500 an acre, plus watering costs — but essential. "The problem is not simply

Fiberglass tree cuffs were used in the early days to protect newly planted trees from bark nibblers like these rare okapi. Tree protection is still necessary, but new materials make cuffs less noticeable.

erosion," Gibbons noted, "but the dangers it causes for the animals — babies falling into ditches or youngsters running and breaking a leg in a small crevice they didn't see."

While determined not to let Mother Nature take its course in terms of erosion, Wild Animal Park officials were equally concerned about the quality of the animals' environment. From the beginning, they sought ways to create exhibits that catered as much as possible to the natural needs of each species and their potential range of behaviors.

Mammal curator Larry Killmar pointed out some subtle things that make an animal feel at home and, as a result, more inclined to reproduce. "One thing was to provide tall feeder poles upon which to hang vegetation for natural browsers like giraffes, elands, and kudus. They can adjust and eat browse that's lying on the ground, but they're much happier reaching up to eat. We also leave tree stumps, so the rhinos can rub their hides, other animals can satisfy territorial instincts by scenting areas with urine, and deer can rub the velvet off their antlers. Then there are animals like the sitatunga (the most aquatic of the antelopes), which need places to go where they can get away from the other species. They like to hide along the stream which runs year-round through the Eastern Africa exhibit, and also down around the lake at the lower end of the exhibit."

Killmar also noted that while erosion control was necessary, and most visitors preferred to see the hills and valleys carpeted with grass, it was critical not to ignore animal preferences. "We have to compromise," he said. "While erosion creates dangerous conditions for babies of some species, we have to leave certain areas in their dry, natural state so that animals who dislike grass or wet areas can still retreat to where they won't feel stressed. Also, mothers of certain species need suitably rough terrain to hide or 'tuck' their babies for several weeks after birth, and if we didn't provide areas that satisfy these anti-predator instincts, we could produce aberrant behavior.

"We'd also be negligent if we didn't consider the practical needs of animals like zebras, which groom themselves by rolling in dust, mostly as a deterrent to insects such as flies. We also maintain barren areas used by groups of bachelor males. We purposely don't enhance these areas with trees or whatever, because we don't want to attract other groups. We want to give the loners a place where they can basically avoid both trouble and interaction with other animals."

"As close to nature as possible" also applies to feeding animals. Keepers use "feeder trees" to elevate browse to a natural level for these Ugandan giraffes.

Behind the Scenes at the San Diego Wild Animal Park

Since its founding, the San Diego Wild Animal Park has joined with the San Diego Zoo to play an indispensible role in the worldwide efforts by zoologists and conservationists to save as many wild animal species as possible from extinction. There's a growing urgency in this mission; for many experts are convinced that by the year 2000, hundreds of species may exist only in zoos, game reserves, and other captive environments. Said general curator Jim Dolan, "We believe that places like the Wild Animal Park, working together with other zoos, offer the best hope of safeguarding these animals."

At the Wild Animal Park, a major emphasis is on species officially classified as "endangered" by the U.S. Department of the Interior or by one of several international conservation agencies. These species are most in need of immediate attention because they have become extinct in the wild or are perilously close, and their fate hinges on efforts to increase their captive populations. Yet *all* reproductive efforts at the Wild Animal Park are important; for wherever animals live wild today, their continued existence is imperiled by mankind's relentless encroachments and short-sighted personal whims.

Deforestation, of course, is the overwhelming problem throughout the world's tropical zones. Fragile natural habitats are being systematically and perhaps irrevocably destroyed as man invades — by building roads, cutting timber, excavating for minerals, or clearing land for farming and grazing.

Even an endangered species living in a habitat safely removed from "civilization" is subject to the threat of poachers, who supply the worldwide demand for products made from dwindling animal populations: stuffed monkeys, crocodile handbags, elephant ivory, zebra-skin wall hangings, snakeskin shoes, and artwork constructed from tropical bird feathers. Leopards, tigers, and jaguars are hunted for their skins;

primates such as gibbons and douc langurs are killed for their meat. Indian and African rhinos are butchered simply for their horns, which are ground into powder for aphrodisiac pills or made into elaborate dagger handles — an expensive male status symbol in North Yemen.

Given these realities, and the fact that securing animals from the wild has become virtually impossible except through rescue efforts, the Wild Animal Park is a vital haven for vanishing wildlife — notably hoofed animals, or ungulates. No other institution has had such breeding success with so many different ungulate species.

"This is the largest collection of hoofed animals that has ever been kept anywhere at one time in a captive-breeding situation," said Jim Dolan. More than 90 such species and subspecies are represented, in addition to birds, primates, and other mammals. Altogether, the Wild Animal Park is home to about 2,200 animals comprising approximately 225 species and subspecies, including 37 endangered species. Nearly all of these species reproduce at the Park, given time and suitable mates, and the survival rate among those born is 80 percent, five times higher than in the wild."

This remarkable success in propagating such a diverse cast of characters is tribute to the Wild Animal Park's increasingly sophisticated management techniques, experience, and collaborative efforts by curators, keepers, veterinarians, and researchers.

The Keepers' Role

The Wild Animal Park keepers are men and women ranging in age from early 20s to the 50s with varied backgrounds — some have college degrees, others arrived with farming or animal-raising experience.

"One thing we all have in common is a love for the animals and for what we're doing," said mammal manager Rich Massena. "We get a real sense of accomplishment out of our jobs." This philosophy is typified by mammal keeper Barbara Schwankl, an Ohio State graduate (her degree is in natural resources with distinction in wildlife management), who said, "I believe in the cause — animal conservation — and I want to do my part."

The keepers are at the forefront of the daily care and observation of the Wild Animal Park's animals. In Nairobi Village, each keeper has his or her string of mammals or birds to care for, while each major exhibit is covered by a two-person team working from a flatbed truck.

Field keepers arrive for work between 6:00 and 6:30 a.m., meeting in front of Rich Massena's trailer, which serves as headquarters for day-to-day mammal operations. After discussing special projects that need attention (for example, immobilizing an animal that will be shipped to another zoo), keepers drive to the food warehouses, load their trucks, and fan out to their respective exhibits. Each exhibit has numerous cement feeders, strategically located to minimize competition among the different species living there and to allow for public viewing from the monorail.

Before distributing food, the keepers' first concern as they enter a field exhibit is injured animals or newborn babies. An effort is made to identify permanently each newborn in order to facilitate future reproduction and maintenance of healthy and viable animal populations.

When a mother is not aggressive toward keepers, initial "processing" — the term for routine care of newborns — is a relatively easy task. The baby is captured, and its umbilicus is soaked with a solution of iodine and water to protect it from neonatal diseases and infection. The baby is then weighed, measured, and inoculated against viruses and infant diseases. Keepers are also able to detect any physical problems that might necessitate hand-raising. Finally, the baby's ears are notched and an identification number is tattooed on one to enable keepers and veterinarians to identify accurately animals in the field from several hundred yards away. It also ensures more precise breeding records in the years to come.

Infant processing is much more difficult and dangerous when certain species are involved — notably the addax and the white-bearded wilde-beest, for mothers are fiercely pro-tective of their young. "The addax are consistently one of the most dangerous animals we have to contend with because they're not intimidated by

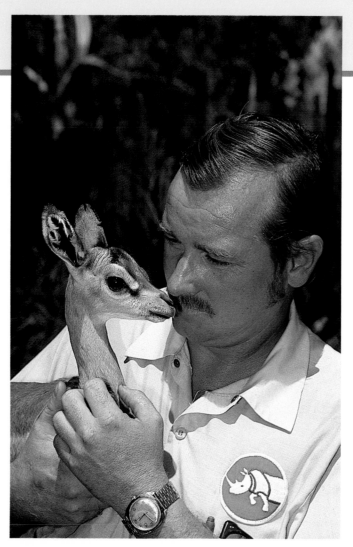

Although endangered in their Sahara native habitat, these addax (Addax nasomaculatus) have been prolific at the Wild Animal Park. Mother addax are fiercely protective of their young.

us whatsoever and they have long corkscrew horns," said curator Larry Killmar. "Mothers with babies often charge the keeper trucks, occasionally putting holes in the sides. Even an aggressive mother whose nearby calf is not involved in a health check will attack us because she feels threatened by our presence."

With most animals, the mother runs away when keepers drive up, and they can spend five or 10 minutes with the baby before turning it loose. But the addax mom stays so close to her baby that the keepers can't even jump out of the truck. Instead, they put a hoisting loop around the baby's neck and pull it safely into the truck for processing. Then they give it back to its mother.

More than 300 babies are born each year in the large exhibits, and most of them join their respective herds. However, certain babies have to be hand-raised at the Animal Care Center in Nairobi Village, for a number of reasons: the baby is neglected or rejected by its mother; keepers determine that a new-

born is too weak to survive in the field, especially if the weather is cold and wet; several herds are so prolific (blackbuck and axis deer, for example) that most babies will eventually be shipped to another zoo. It's easier and less stressful on the animals to crate them at the Animal Care Center than to tranquilize them in the field.

As field keepers "feed out" their exhibit in the morning, they also count the animals. This daily inventory is an important part of overall animal management at the Wild Animal Park. Through it, keepers maintain familiarity with each species and, thus, the ability to anticipate and assess animal behavior. Said assistant mammal manager Randy Rieches, "You learn to see the subtle changes from day to day that are a clue to some problem developing with the animal's health or a behavior change, such as aggression toward another animal."

Using binoculars if necessary, keepers make a visual evaluation each day of as many individual animals as

20

possible, checking for signs of diarrhea; limping, cuts or lacerations that might have occurred in a fight; developing pregnancies; or impending births. Over time, keepers learn an animal's history and its particular habits (such as whether or not it is inclined to fight), and curators and veterinarians rely on these trained judgments.

Keepers are also called upon to take seat-of-the-pants action to save an animal caught in a life-threatening situation. Randy Rieches and keeper Gerry Bender were in the Eastern Africa exhibit when a freak thunder-and-lightning storm suddenly hit. In particular, a lightning bolt struck just outside of Northern Africa, frightening the herd of Ugandan giraffes, who began running loops around their exhibit.

"One of the giraffes was only about two weeks old and had just been released into the exhibit with mom from a protective boma," Rieches recalled. "The first time around the exhibit, the giraffes skirted one of the ponds, hidden behind a hill; they were familiar with the exhibit and knew it was there. On the next loop, though, the giraffe calf went up the hill and then right down into the pond, which is about 18 feet deep. She didn't know it was there. She tried to swim, but a giraffe can't swim, and she flailed about until she was in the middle of the pond, then she went down."

The two keepers ran to the pond. Rieches jumped in and swam to where the giraffe had disappeared, while Bender stayed on the bank and looked for bubbles. "When I finally found her," said Rieches, "I pushed her head up out of the water, but with her long neck, I had to stay underwater in order to keep her head up. Somehow we got her to shore, but she wasn't breathing. We turned her upside down on the bank, got her head down, and started pumping her heart and massaging her abdomen. That forced a lot of water out and started her breathing again. We then pushed her back up on her feet and found her mom. She was really sick for about two days, but she nursed and recovered."

The axis deer or chital (Cervus a. axis) *does not lose its spots, like most deer species, which have spotted coats only in infancy. This deer, native to India, is an exceptional swimmer.*

21

More than 15 different species of mammals peacefully coexist in the Eastern Africa enclosure, including this endangered northern white rhinoceros, Ugandan giraffes, and white-bearded wildebeest.

Animal Management

"The first five years out here," said curator Larry Killmar, "our main concern was to establish the Wild Animal Park and build breeding groups; we had to prove that we could do it. The next five years, we focused on successfully maintaining everything and adding to the collection. But now the emphasis is on closer management of each species so that we maintain good numbers, viable bloodlines, and self-sustaining populations — without overpopulating any particular species or exhibit."

The continuing population growth at the Park — thanks primarily to ongoing breeding successes — has forced keepers and curators not only to monitor the effects that overcrowding has on an entire exhibit, but also to anticipate when it could produce a problem within a particular species.

"We're continually assessing the number of animals we should keep — particularly males — in order to minimize conflicts and promote continued reproduction," said Killmar. "Our goal has always been to have a self-sustaining animal population, and we're at that point now with most of our herds."

One danger to avoid is allowing one male to remain too long as the dominant breeder within a species, which can weaken the genetic line and bring about inbreeding problems. When a sire loses his genetic usefulness, Killmar searches for a male from a new bloodline, ideally through a zoological institution having a suitable male for exchange. "Sometimes it's impossible to find a new male — all the available ones are related — so then we just try to maintain the best possible mix we can," Killmar explained.

Keepers and curators also prevent potentially harmful skirmishes by removing young male challengers before they try to overthrow a herd's dominant male, especially when the latter is a proven breeder, is still in his prime, and is an endangered species. This philosophy was applied to the Indian rhinos in the Asian Plains exhibit, where keepers removed Lasai's son, Pandu, just before his third birthday. Lasai was chasing Pandu, who thought it was a game. But the two were heading for a serious confrontation, and Pandu could have been badly hurt. Even with 60 acres, there simply wasn't enough room in the exhibit for Pandu to escape.

Over the years, most animals in the five major exhibits have learned to coexist peacefully, as originally intended. Yet, since new species and animals are continually introduced, keepers must constantly monitor animal interactions, interpreting and anticipating aggressive behavior that could suddenly prove fatal.

One example involved introducing five Sunda wild boars into the Asian Plains. The Indian gaurs took offense to the new residents and, after several nasty confrontations, the boars were moved to the Asian Waterhole to ensure their survival. "We have water buffalo in this exhibit," said Randy Rieches, "but they are such complacent animals, they befriended the boars. They traveled together and even slept together." In fact, monorail visitors often mistook the boars for offspring of the buffalo.

Animal conflicts are inevitable at the Wild Animal Park, given a captive situation that so closely approximates nature. But considering the number of animals involved, there have been relatively few fights resulting in serious injury or death. One reason is that keepers often are able to intercede on behalf of an animal in trouble.

For instance, one morning as keepers entered Eastern Africa, they spotted a male ostrich stuck in the mud at the edge of the large pond. The breeding season was approaching and apparently the older male ostrich in the group had chased his rival into the water. Five keepers were needed to handle the rescue, as they tied ropes around the ostrich's body and then

pulled him to shore.

Then, there are those times when everyone is happily fooled by the results of an introduction. Once, a male dromedary camel was moved to the Northern Africa exhibit, which features an impressive herd of addax, and keepers feared that the females, who are fiercely protective mothers, would gore the camel if he innocently approached a mother and her baby. While keepers were poised to come to the camel's rescue, the addax, as well as the addra gazelles, fled to the back of the exhibit at first sight of this strange one-humped creature. They hadn't seen a camel before, and they stayed well away for the next two days, not even converging at night to eat from their feeders. Finally, they worked up enough courage — and hunger — to risk drawing near the camel, but not without closely watching his every move.

Domestic water buffalo (Bubalis arnee f. bubalis) *cool off in the deep waters of the Asian Waterhole. Domesticated about 3000 B.C., water buffalo are widely used throughout the world for farming and as dairy cattle.*

23

Transporting animals between zoos around the world is a real challenge, especially for delicate or large animals like this Asiatic elephant.

Animal Acquisition

Since zoos and animal parks can no longer rely upon the wild to bolster their collections, they must depend upon themselves — individually and collectively — to create and maintain collections that are conservation-oriented, reproductively viable, and pleasing to visitors. Responsible curators know that numerous captive-breeding groups of a particular endangered species must exist before they can breathe easier about its fate. Only by trading excess animals, swapping unrelated animals, and arranging breeding loans can zoos minimize in-breeding problems and build a species' captive population to the point where it can withstand any future setbacks.

"It's unrealistic for us (zoos) to think that we'll get many animals from the wilds of Africa and Asia in the future," noted curator Larry Killmar. "Even when animals do become

available, the cost, the paperwork, and the regulations involved in shipping them are just staggering. That's why we must look to *ourselves* (the Wild Animal Park) as the wild, where we strive to produce as many animals as possible so we can meet our own needs on a continuing basis, while supplying other zoos here and abroad."

Virtually all animals acquired by the Wild Animal Park are obtained through trades or on breeding loans, and Killmar estimates that 50 percent of the animals who leave the Park are traded. "We'll sell if the opportunity presents itself," he said, "but most people prefer to trade for an animal we need, such as when we exchanged 35 blackbuck antelopes and 35 axis deer for two dromedary camels."

The Park maintains a list of surplus animals for sale or trade, while pursuing up to 15 different species at one time — either individual animals to fill a specific need, or a new breeding group for the overall collection.

Meanwhile, the Wild Animal Park is actively involved in a program organized by the American Association of Zoological Parks and Aquariums (AAZPA), called the Species Survival Plan (SSP). The SSP, conceived in 1980, is a cooperative effort among zoos to manage long-term captive-breeding programs for endangered species. Thus far, 31 species (mostly large mammals) have been designated for SSP attention, and the Wild Animal Park is involved in SSP programs for gorillas, Indian rhinos, Przewalski's horses, Arabian oryx, Grevy's zebras, Asian lions, and okapis, among others.

Developing each SSP is an enormous undertaking. It means identifying zoos which have a particular species, inventorying their specimens, determining genetic background, and developing a coordinated strategy for the entire North American captive population. International cooperation is sought for many species, but the SSP program is mainly an effort of North American zoos.

The goal is to build captive populations and prevent inbreeding by matching unrelated individuals for mating whenever possible, thus diversifying bloodlines.

Jim Dolan cited the Grevy's zebras as an example of how the Wild Animal

Park works with the SSP to help the entire species in the U.S. "We know we've bred too long with the two males in our different herds (one major herd on exhibit and a smaller one off exhibit), so we've requested through SSP that they find us two males in exchange."

Considerable attention and concern is given to the endangered species living at the Wild Animal Park, because curators know their success with virtually all resident species has long-range implications. Even for those species appearing to be "secure" in the wild today, conditions can change swiftly — given the effects of long-term drought, war, or simply the inexorable crush of human population demands. An endangered species in Africa, for instance, may be making population gains in national parks and protected reserves, but losing numbers in the wild, such as in Uganda, where warfare has raged for years.

"I don't think the Wild Animal Park's role can afford to change," commented Jim Dolan. "In fact, the focus on reproduction should become stronger, because conditions don't get any better. Desertification in Africa, for example, is claiming more and more of the land there, and population growth there and in Asia is outrageous."

Thus, while the Wild Animal Park strives for continued reproductive success with the animals now in its collection, the curators keep broadening the horizon, trying to add new species every year. One of Dolan's goals is to achieve a greater balance of the overall collection, by providing space for breeding groups of smaller rare mammals from rain forest environments — in his words, to "increase the scope of the place by building some intimate exhibits in which we can deal with smaller mammals who deserve as much attention as the large ungulates." Added Larry Killmar, "We have so many different species now that we can put together a package of surplus animals to trade for those that were once too expensive for us to obtain."

Veterinary Care

Veterinary care at the Wild Animal Park, directed by Dr. James Oosterhuis, involves a daily mixture of emergency "calls" and tending to various husbandry demands within the collection, including preventive medicine and ongoing research projects as time and opportunity allow.

"With only two veterinarians here at any one time," said Oosterhuis, "the Park is too large for us to make the rounds every day, so we're basically a fire-engine type of practice, responding to the most urgent cases first."

Oosterhuis arrives at the Park hospital between 6:30 and 7:00 a.m. He first checks the status of injured or ailing animals being housed in special stalls

Through breeding success at the Wild Animal Park and other preserves around the world, the southern white rhinoceros (Ceratotherium s. simum) has been rescued from the brink of extinction. More than 20 of these rhinos live in the Park's Southern Africa exhibit.

25

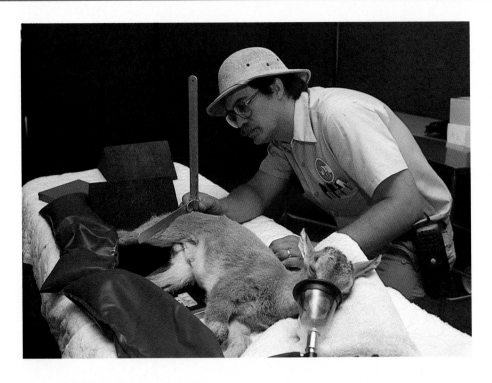

Above: A staff keeps the animals in good health. Here, Dr. Oosterhuis x-rays an injured leg on this baby markhor.

Right: The white-bearded gnu or wildebeest (Connochaetes taurinus albojubatus) is one of nature's oddest-looking creatures. In Africa, these antelopes migrate in huge herds for thousands of miles.

at the hospital, as well as babies being hand-reared in the Animal Care Center and the Infant Isolation Unit. "When you're hand-rearing 120 babies a year," he noted, "there's invariably some animal who has diarrhea, an eating problem, or a minor injury."

As keepers begin their feed runs and survey the species in their exhibits, they report any special findings or abnormalities to the veterinarians by walkie-talkie. "We have a major injury once or twice a week, especially now as the collection ages and we have a greater number of older animals," Oosterhuis said.

If no early-morning emergencies arise, the veterinarians truck to an exhibit to handle an immobilization or two before the day heats up. "We probably immobilize more animals each year than any other place in the world, but it's necessary."

Veterinarians use a dart gun for most field immobilizations; and getting close enough to the target animal to make a safe, accurate shot can be an exasperating, time-consuming effort for the vet and several teams of keepers. Once the animal has been darted, teamwork is necessary to guide the animal to an appropriate area for treatment before the drug takes effect.

Keepers must be prepared if the darted animal begins to run around the exhibit. Eventually, the drug renders it totally defenseless, and keepers must protect the animal from a rival who would take advantage of its weakened condition. Occasionally, an immobilized animal instinctively heads for a pond. If keepers are unable to cut him off in time, they have to enter the water, grab the animal, and guide it to safety. When an animal has been drugged, it loses control over its swallowing reflex; and if it submerges even for a few seconds, it can get water in its lungs and die. These risks are necessary, though, to manage such a diverse, populous animal collection.

Under certain circumstances, medical treatment and even some surgery is done in the field — ideally, inside a boma, which provides shelter and protection during treatment and the recovery period. In most cases, however, the animal is placed in a crate or the back of a flatbed truck and transported to the hospital for treatment.

Even on a day when no emergencies occur, Oosterhuis and his staff are faced with a long list of animals needing treatment. "I go through 16 keeper reports each day," said Oosterhuis, "circling and highlighting the problems they have observed, or something they suspect is wrong with the animal, and I try to put a priority on what should be done. Fortunately, some of these things clear up on their own." Preventive medicine at the Wild Animal Park includes dental work, vitamin supplements, inoculations, vaccinations, routine parasite checks, hoof trims, post-natal exams, and routine physical exams.

In addition to medical care and health maintenance, Oosterhuis and his staff assist the keepers in ongoing research projects. For instance, for the elephant breeding program, keepers were collecting urine from female Asian elephants every day, to analyze each animal's hormone levels and determine when she would be in estrus and receptive to the bull, Ranchipur. Researchers also know from blood samples when a female is pregnant. The elephants were also involved in an ongoing nutritional study, testing the effectiveness of a new vitamin-mineral supplement pellet.

Two domes on its head and small ears characterize the popular Asiatic elephant (Elephas maximus indicus). *The Park's herd provides education and entertainment through shows and rides.*

Research Efforts

Efforts to increase reproduction and survival rates at the Wild Animal Park are receiving important contributions from the Zoological Society's world-renowned research department based at the San Diego Zoo. Supported by experts in behavior, genetics, endocrinology, virology, and pathology, Park personnel are using increasingly sophisticated methods to strengthen the captive status of such disparate species as California condors and Asian elephants.

A prime example is the extensive research program on the social behavior and reproductive physiology of South African cheetahs in captivity. This program has yielded more than 48 cubs since 1970, and a procedure to implant an estrogen pump has been tested and could enhance other breeding programs.

The Wild Animal Park acquired 10 wild cheetahs in 1970. They provided one of the Park's early success stories by giving birth to the first surviving cheetahs in the U.S. late that year. One behavioral discovery was that reproduction improves with complete segregation of males and females for most of the year, letting them share an enclosure only when the female is in estrus. Later, Zoo researchers learned that strong mate preferences exist in both sexes, and that the chances of successful breeding are enhanced if females can be selective when they come into estrus.

With a species as severely endangered as the cheetah — about 10,000 in the wild and 200 in captivity in North America — Zoological Society behaviorist Dr. Donald Lindburg knows that it is crucial for every animal of breeding age to be utilized, regardless of the animal's behavioral or reproductive problems. Thus, he is encouraged by a breakthrough method that induces ovulation and enhances reproductive rates of females which were not conceiving, or not conceiving as well as they should, or showing no interest in breeding.

Early in 1984, a hormonal pump was inserted into Nyrie, who hadn't bred for two years. It was hoped this thumb-sized under-the-skin implant (modifying a technique used successfully in infertile women) would stimulate ovulation and begin estrus. The implant worked, Nyrie bred, and three months later gave birth to two cubs — the first wild carnivore litter ever produced by this method in the U.S.

Lindburg's next strategy is artificial insemination in females which remain intolerant of males. "We have a hand-raised female, Sheba, who's in her reproductive prime, but has never displayed any interest in males," explained Lindburg. "So we're obtaining semen at regular intervals from a hand-raised male, Pesach, and we'll use it when we have Sheba's ovaries primed. Artificial insemination, in this case, would be used only if Sheba continues to be intolerant of males after she has been hormonally primed. Without these efforts, the chances of her ever being a mother are pretty remote."

These attempts to expand the potential breeding program are critical to the cheetah's future, noted Lindburg, "because there are many female cheetahs sitting in zoos that just don't show any signs of interest in sexual activity. We still have a lot to learn about cheetahs, but once we understand all the social and physical aspects, our collection will benefit and we'll be able to pass along important knowledge to other zoos and wildlife parks."

The research department also plays an important role in the breeding program for the Wild Animal Park's Asiatic elephants, an endangered species,

which acquired a $360,000 facility in October 1984 to enhance breeding and mothering.

This state-of-the-art breeding facility includes a barn that provides shelter for up to 10 cows, including a maternity stall; a separate night barn for the resident bull, Ranchipur; and an outdoor bull yard that can be used for breeding or sectioned off as a nursery where mother, baby, and an "auntie" can exercise and get fresh air before being placed among the herd. Adjacent to the maternity stall is a keepers' "apartment" unit where keepers and veterinarians can conduct 24-hour-a-day surveillance of expectant and new mothers and have quick, easy access for specialized care.

The breeding program itself actually began with the selection of two cows — 30-year-old Cookie and 19-year-old Carol. In order for researchers to pinpoint each female's estrus cycle, keepers collected blood and urine samples from the prospective cows several times a week for three months. Analysis led researchers to suggest Carol as the first participant in the breeding program, and keepers began taking daily blood and urine samples, hoping to learn exactly when she would ovulate.

Left: The South African cheetah (Acinonyx j. jubatus) is another example of endangered breeding success for the Wild Animal Park. More than 50 cubs have been born.

Right: The South African cheetah is not an easy species to breed. Zoological Society researchers work closely with the animals to encourage pairing at appropriate times.

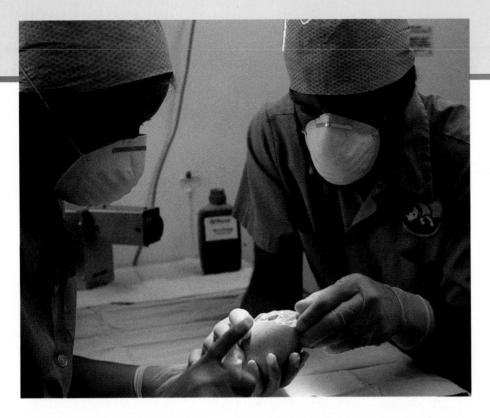

Above: With the precision of surgeons, keepers peel away pieces of shell from a hatching California condor chick. In the wild, parents may pick off shell fragments with their beaks.

Right: A California condor (Gymnogyps californianus) juvenile tests its wings in short practice flights within its spacious condorminium. Condors attain their adult wingspan of nearly nine feet at six months. Inset: A California condor hand puppet is used to feed and preen this two-week-old condor chick. For several years, eggs have been taken from the central California wilds for hatching at the Park. The eventual plan is a captive breeding program, with selected birds released back into the wild.

Meanwhile, keepers acquainted Carol with Ranchipur and vice versa; they backed her up to the bull's slightly-ajar door, and he gave her a normal "sniff test" with his trunk. Carol was then led into a transfer area in the main compound for a formal introduction to Ranchipur and another sniff test. The introduction went well, and the two spent the rest of the day in Ranchipur's outdoor compound.

Researchers monitored this pairing seven days a week — from 8:30 a.m. until late afternoon, when the elephants returned to their respective barns — as they sought to link their behavioral studies with monitoring of the female's ovarian function. "We want to learn the parameters of courtship and how these are influenced by the female's hormonal state," explained Lindburg. "These insights should improve the success of future matings."

Overseeing the elephant collection at the Wild Animal Park and the San Diego Zoo is Briton Alan Roocroft, whose dedication to their present well-being and ultimate survival is deep-rooted. He left school at 14 and began working with elephants at the Manchester Zoo. At 22, he spent a year in Sri Lanka, immersing himself in elephant life, then worked 10 years as a keeper with the Hagenbeck Zoo in Hamburg, West Germany. He came to the Wild Animal Park in 1983.

Since Asian elephants can no longer be exported directly from Asia, and only nine Asian elephants have entered the U.S. legally since 1974, Roocroft knows that pressure is on the Park to have as many births as possible in the coming years, to meet the Society's needs and for shipment to other zoos. Only four other institutions currently breed Asian elephants in captivity — the Portland, Miami Metro, and Bronx zoos, and Circus World in Florida.

But, as Roocroft points out, "We only want to have two Asian elephant babies on the grounds at one time, in order to give them our best attention. Once our two cows are pregnant, we want to stagger future births and return our focus to the African elephants to breed them again. The African elephant, in fact, is disappearing faster in the wild now than the Asian." The African's numbers continue to decline despite the protection offered them in safari parks and game preserves, and attempts to reduce illegal ivory dealing.

The California Condor: The Race Against Extinction

While most of the animals at the Wild Animal Park live within view of visitors, several endangered species are maintained off-exhibit to minimize their exposure to humans and maximize captive breeding efforts. One example is the California condor, North America's largest bird, which is virtually extinct in its habitat north of Los Angeles.

Alarmed by the condor's steadily declining numbers, federal, state, and conservation officials launched a Condor Recovery Program in 1979. Three years later, when just 19 condors existed in the wild (plus three in captivity), the California Fish and Game Commission approved a rescue effort that entailed radio-tagging birds in the wild, taking eggs from their cliffside nests for artificial incubation, and captive breeding at the Wild Animal Park and the Los Angeles Zoo. A condor mother will "double-clutch," or lay a second egg, when her first egg is lost to predators, including biologists; this obviously increases the number of potential condor births each year.

Four chicks were hatched at the San

Diego Zoo in the program's first year, nine more hatchlings followed by mid-1985, and four young birds were taken from the wild. With about 20 condors now in captivity, project officials will strive to create breeding pairs, to assure a continuing supply of eggs. Eventually, selected pairs may be released into the wild, but for now, the California condor's survival must rely on captive breeding efforts. In fact, officials fear that the wild population is less than 10.

The condor facility at the Wild Animal Park is located on an isolated hill, overlooking the Asian Plains exhibit, and includes six large wire-covered flight cages, or "condorminiums."

Returning Animals to the Wild

"Nobody is going to deny that the best place for wild animals to live is in their native environment," said Dr. Jim Dolan, general curator of mammals. "But when that habitat is rapidly disappearing or a species is being decimated by poachers, the only humane solution is to give representative animals a protected environment where they can survive. Then hope for the day things settle down and sanity prevails and you can reintroduce this species to its former

Above: The Arabian oryx (Oryx leucoryx) symbolizes the Wild Animal Park's goal of preserving an endangered species through reproduction, combined with returning animals to their native habitat. More than 130 Arabian oryx have been born at the Park and 35 returned to Middle East preserves.

Right: Southern white rhinoceros (Ceratotherium s. simum) silhouetted during a summer sunset. The southern white rhino is the symbol of breeding success at the Wild Animal Park.

habitat. When and if that day comes, at least there will be animals available that can go back into the wild or into protected reserves where they evolved."

This major objective of the Wild Animal Park has been achieved with the Arabian oryx, a beautiful sand-colored antelope with two long, straight horns.

The Arabian oryx once roamed Middle East deserts, but their numbers grew increasingly scarce by the early 1960s, victimized by "sport" hunters using submachine guns and high-powered rifles from trucks and helicopters. In 1963, conservationists gathered together the eight remaining wild oryx to form a captive breeding group at the Phoenix Zoo. When they proved to be prolific breeders, six animals were transferred to the Wild Animal Park in 1972.

Over the next 12 years, 134 babies were born at the Park, and other breeding groups were started at six zoos in the U.S. and Europe. Their ultimate survival ensured, the Park returned 35 oryx to reserves in the Middle East, where some live free in their native homeland.

Sixteen Arabian oryx from the Wild Animal Park were sent to Oman from 1980 to 1984, after the Sultan extracted a promise from the Beduins not to shoot them. The oryx live on the Jiddat al Harasis, a 19,305-square-mile vegetated plateau having distinct natural boundaries but no protective fencing. The local Beduins, the Harasis tribe, guard the oryx from poachers and take great pride in overseeing the project's success, because the Arabian oryx is an integral part of their cultural heritage — in Harasis legend, it embodies the strength and power of all that lives.

The oryx live at large in the desert and are completely independent of human influence, except for the guards who prevent poaching. The oryx no longer rely on humans for food, water, and shelter; and, on their own, they have established two herds, each with a dominant male. Some calves have been born.

A large herd of Arabian oryx still resides at the Wild Animal Park, and visitors can see them from the Wgasa Bush Line monorail.

Nairobi Village Map

FUCHSIA GARDEN

EPIPHYLLUM HOUSE

MONORAIL BOARDING

NYALA

ELEPHANT OVERLOOK

CONIFER ARBORETUM

KILIMANJARO TRAIL

LIONS

ASIAN ELEPHANTS

AFRICAN ELEPHANTS

TIGERS

ELEPHANT SHOW

CHEETAHS

CALIFORNIA NATIVE PLANT TRAIL

PICNIC AREA

HERB GARDEN

PUMZIKA POINT

SAVANNAH PICNIC GROVE

EASTERN AFRICA

PARKING

VILLAGE
AMPHITHEATER

ANIMAL
ANTICS SHOW

INFORMATION

EXIT
CAMERA
HUT

FIRST AID

AVIARY

THE PLANT
TRADER

T-SHIRT
SHOP

MONORAIL
TICKETS

ENTRANCE

WGASA
BUSH LINE

FISHING CAMP

CONGO
KITCHEN

BAZAAR

THORN TREE
TERRACE

ANIMAL CARE
CENTER

GORILLA
GROTTO

GAZELLE

PRIMATE
ISLE

PETTING KRAAL

ALOE TRAIL

ANTELOPE

COVERED
WALKWAY

PAVILION

ELEPHANT
WASH

PICNIC
AREA

BRIDGE
OF BIRDS

MOMBASA
COOKER

START OF
HIKING TRAIL

BIRD SHOW

ELEPHANT
RIDES

MONORAIL
UNLOADING

SAMBURU
BARBECUE
TERRACE

TROPICAL AMERICA

AUSTRALIAN
RAIN FOREST

HANUMAN
LANGURS

KILIMANJARO TRAIL

MAHALA
AMPHITHEATER

Right: Long limbs and necks enable the Somali gerenuk (Litocranius walleri sclateri) *to browse on tall bushes and trees. Gerenuk is a Somali word for giraffe-necked, which aptly describes these rare and delicate gazelles.*

Far right: The Park's expansive enclosures allow large animals, like these Ugandan giraffes (Giraffa camelopardalis rothschildi), *plenty of room to run and raise their young.*

Seeing the San Diego Wild Animal Park

Concealed barriers divide the principal exhibits into five main biogeographical areas: the savannas of eastern Africa, the Asian plains, the deserts of northern Africa, the Asian waterholes, and the savannas of southern Africa. Animals living in these exhibits roam freely, forming herd hierarchies and pursuing daily routines much as they would in the wild, while peacefully co-existing with numerous other species. Unlike traditional zoos, the Wild Animal Park is designed to give visitors an insight into these various behaviors, from mothers giving birth within view of the passing monorail to deer, goats, and sheep clashing horns during their rutting seasons.

The Major Habitats

Eastern Africa

Traveling on the monorail, this is the first exhibit visitors see after passing the African and Asian elephants. Numerous types of antelope live in this 125-acre exhibit, including roan antelope, Kenyan impala, defassa waterbuck, fringe-eared oryx, Nile lechwe, Patterson's eland, Uganda kob, and Speke's sitatunga. They co-exist with a variety of neighbors such as Cape buffalo, a northern white rhino, Roosevelt's gazelle, and white-bearded gnu or wildebeest, which roam in a large herd, much as they would across the Serengeti Plain of Tanzania and Kenya.

A herd of Ugandan giraffes provides a striking, graceful presence in this exhibit, whether ambling across the flatlands, reaching up to munch browse, or simply peering at monorail visitors who pass nearby. Through 1984, more than 20 giraffes had been born at the Wild Animal Park (quite an accomplishment for a species with a 14-month gestation), most sired by the majestic, dark-colored Blackjack.

35

Above: Beautifully ringed horns and an erect mane characterize the Angolan roan antelope (Hippotragus equinus cottoni). The third largest member of the antelope family, the roan is rarely seen outside of Africa.

Previous page: African bush elephants (Loxodonta a. africana) are the largest land mammal. The Wild Animal Park is one of the few zoos to record births of this endangered species.

At one point, Blackjack was ousted as herd sire by another male, Kidenoi, acquired from the Bronx Zoo. Blackjack chose to become an outcast, a solitary animal who distanced himself from the other giraffes. "Kidenoi was a successful breeder," said curator Larry Killmar, "but we didn't like the light color of his offspring — we preferred Blackjack's color patterns — so we shipped Kidenoi to another zoo. The minute he was gone, Blackjack came right back in and resumed his dominant role."

Outside of Nairobi Village, the Eastern Africa exhibit has the largest collection of birds at the Wild Animal Park. In 1985, these included white-backed pelicans, ground hornbills, Goliath herons, and white-backed vultures (both species are rare in American bird collections), and about 25 lesser flamingos. The flamingos live along the large pond at the lower end of the exhibit, just below the monorail tracks, and Park visitors will eventually be able to watch the flamingos march in sync with wings spread during breeding season and raise their chicks.

Asian Plains

As the monorail moves up the valley from Eastern Africa, it circles the 60-acre Asian Plains and offers visitors a panoramic view of numerous species native to Asia — from endangered animals such as barasingha deer, Indian gaur, and Javan rusa deer to herds of Persian goitered gazelle, axis deer, and blackbuck antelope.

Living in the upper end of this exhibit is a prized family of Indian rhinos, headed by Lasai, one of the Wild Animal Park's most prominent animal personalities.

Born at the Basel Zoo in Switzerland in 1962 and acquired by the Zoological Society of San Diego in 1963, Lasai sired five surviving offspring at the Wild Animal Park through 1985, a significant contribution to a species that numbers approximately 1,300 in the wilds of India and Nepal and barely 200 in zoos and wildlife parks worldwide. "The Indian rhinos are an important symbol for our

role here at the Park," said general curator Jim Dolan. "We give them living space and a lot of special attention because of their status in the wild and the difficulty in maintaining them in captivity."

Establishing an Indian rhino breeding program at the Wild Animal Park has been a long, demanding, and oftentimes frustrating struggle. The project began in 1971 when Lasai was transferred to the Park from the Zoo, where he had been living unsuccessfully with Jaypuri. There wasn't enough space at the Zoo, and he was overly aggressive to his intended mate, so breeding never occurred.

After Lasai adjusted to his new home at the Wild Animal Park, Jaypuri was brought in. This time, all went well between them. They had two offspring, but both died soon after birth — a costly loss for a species with a gestation of 16 months. Finally, Gainda was born in March 1978 and survived, as keepers maintained a 24-hour watch in the first critical weeks following birth. A male, Pandu, arrived in 1980, followed by three more males, Tezpur, Jorhat, and Gurkha.

Meanwhile, the Wild Animal Park acquired a young male from the Hyderabad Zoo in India, which represents a valuable new bloodline. The price was stiff — $60,000 for the animal, shipping costs, and various permits, all paid by a private donor. The Wild Animal Park has no guarantee that the bull will be a successful breeder, but gambles must be taken to maintain a viable breeding program. The next effort is to raise funds to build an exhibit solely for Indian rhinos (just across the monorail, below Eastern Africa) that can house a second family unit.

The most conspicuous feature of the ellipsen waterbuck (Kobus e. ellipsiprymnus) *is the white elliptical ring on its rump. These water-loving antelopes are native to central and southern Africa.*

Top: Herds of scimitar-horned oryx (Oryx gazella dammah) *once roamed northern Africa, but now their numbers are threatened by overhunting for their magnificent horns.*

Bottom: The slender-horned gazelle (Gazella l. leptoceros) *is close to extinction in the wilds of northern Africa. Only 100 exist in zoos and preserves worldwide.*

Northern Africa

When the monorail leaves the Asian Plains, it passes above Eastern Africa on the right while the Northern Africa exhibit stretches across a grassy hillside to the left. The 30-acre Northern Africa exhibit is home to two of the Wild Animal Park's most handsome species — the addra gazelle, which has a white coat with striking red coloration on the neck, shoulders, and back; and the scimitar-horned oryx, with its great sweeping horns. Both species are endangered in the wild but fare well in captivity.

Another eye-catching species is the addax, a desert antelope with horns having a slight corkscrew spiral and a coat that turns brilliant white in summer. The addax once roamed the Sahara, but is now endangered due to overhunting and is restricted to several uninhabited areas in the southern Sahara. They breed well in captivity, and several shipments have been sent from the Wild Animal Park to reserves in the Middle East.

The most endangered residents in this exhibit may be the slender-horned gazelles, which are feared to be near extinction in their war-torn habitat — the deserts of Libya and Egypt.

The slender-horned gazelles pose a baffling challenge for Wild Animal Park curators and keepers as they strive to increase the captive population, which totalled just 75 in mid-1985. The gazelles have had more than 190 births since 1972, but the mortality rate is exceptionally high, due to frailty, inbreeding (all slender-horned gazelles in captivity descend from a founding population of just five animals), and difficulty in hand-raising babies which have been rejected by their mothers. Few mothers take care of their own offspring, because they were hand-raised themselves — a frustrating cycle that is difficult to break. Orphaned babies won't eat unless approached just the right way, and they cannot be force-fed.

Nearly all slender-horned gazelles in captivity today belong to the Wild Animal Park, with groups on loan to a half-dozen zoos in the U.S. and Europe. "We hope that with the different groups now going, we can exchange animals and increase the variability within the gene pool," said Jim Dolan.

Southern Africa

As the monorail swings to the left and leaves the Eastern Africa valley behind, visitors come upon the 90-acre Southern Africa exhibit spreading below on the right. This is home for the Wild Animal Park's herd of about 20 southern white rhinos, by far the largest group in the U.S. and symbolic of the animal's remarkable comeback in game reserves and in captivity.

The herd was once presided over by the bull Mandhla, but another male was introduced in 1984 to start a new bloodline. Since the species now seems secure, their cousins, the black rhinos, must become the focus of rescue efforts — in the wild as well as in captivity. The total African population of black rhinoceroses has declined to an estimated 8,000, and the number is falling sharply as the animals fall prey to poachers.

The Wild Animal Park has pinned hopes on a young pair, Nicki and Nanuki (Mwaniki and Nanyuki), growing up in the Southern Africa exhibit. "They appear to be doing really well," observed assistant mammal manager Randy Rieches, "but they're truck hounds and they cause a lot of destruction and mischief. Nanuki, the only black rhino born at the Park, was hand-raised and is still attached to humans, so she's always bothering us, getting in everybody's way all the time. Nicki, who came from another zoo, picked up all her tricks and now they're double trouble. One day, we left a long garden hose in a boma, and they found it and ate the whole thing. They're always looking for new things to play with like that."

As in southern Africa itself, a striking variety of wildlife abounds in this exhibit, from springbok, blesbok, Cape eland, and sable antelope to black wildebeest, Hartmann's mountain zebra, Cape buffalo, and ostrich, the largest living bird. On a hillside just below the monorail is a special enclosure for the greater kudu, which were separated from the others in the hope that "a place of their own" would be more conducive to breeding. This beautiful animal is the second-largest member of the antelope group, standing about five feet high at the shoulder, but is extremely shy and wary of other animals.

Top: With youngsters underfoot, the parents of these South African ostrich (Struthio camelus australis) chicks must keep watch for rhinos and other large animals that share their exhibit.

Bottom: The male greater kudu (Tragelaphus strepsiceros strepsiceros) has spectacular spiral horns. Because of their shy nature, greater kudus occupy a separate enclosure.

39

Top: The first baby ever born at the Park was a Formosan sika deer (Cervus nippon taiouanus). Since then, 100 births of this endangered species have increased its population.

Right: A Sumatran tiger (Panthera tigris sumatrae) prowls through the dense vegetation in its expansive Wild Animal Park exhibit. This endangered feline has reproduced well in the Park.

Asian Waterhole

Located at the easternmost corner of the Wild Animal Park's developed land, this 35-acre boulder-strewn, heavily irrigated enclosure offers numerous hiding places for resident animals — notably exotic deer species — who fare better when they have access to private areas.

"We have to deal with a philosophical problem in this exhibit," said curator Larry Killmar. "Some people complain because they have a hard time seeing all the animals from the monorail. But this exhibit functions wonderfully for those animals that need shelter from constant public view. We can never overlook that if we expect to maximize reproduction of all our species."

One species that has been officially classified as endangered is the Formosan sika deer, a subspecies of sika deer, now extinct in the wild from excessive hunting in the deep mountain forests of Taiwan. Fortunately, more than 400 animals exist in captivity throughout the world, and they are reproducing well, with 100 births at the Wild Animal Park.

Park officials hope that the protective features of this exhibit — rocky hideouts and grassy nooks and crannies — will offer a stimulating refuge for the five Timor rusa deer who arrived via England in 1984. "This is the first group exhibited in this country since 1904," said Larry Killmar. "They've found their niche in the Asian Waterhole, so we're hoping to see offspring."

Special Exhibits

Sumatran Tigers

The two small groups of Sumatran tigers residing in view of the monorail and hikers along the Kilimanjaro Trail represent a patient, persistent effort by the Wild Animal Park to save yet another endangered species. Only a few hundred animals remain in the wild, and an estimated 225 exist in captivity. The Park houses the largest captive group in the U.S. — six adult tigers and a female cub named Masurai, who was born in May 1984, five years

after a group of juvenile tigers arrived from Tierpark Berlin in East Germany. This was the Wild Animal Park's first successful tiger birth, and it was a close call.

"This was the second pregnancy for the mother, Talu, and both times we had to do a Caesarean section," said mammal manager Rich Massena. "The first time she had two stillborn cubs, and the second time there was one stillborn and one live cub. The veterinarian and the keepers had to work hard to get it going, and it was really a happy occasion when they saw her breathe and start moving around."

Since Talu was unable to care for Masurai, the cub was hand-raised at the Animal Care Center in Nairobi Village. But within months, she was successfully introduced to her parents in the tiger bedrooms, then to the other tigers that inhabit the wooded six-acre enclosure. This exhibit allows for the seclusion needed by the tigers, which are solitary animals, and provides ample room for their offspring to grow and thrive.

Births of Asiatic lion (Panthera leo persica) cubs are significant, since barely 300 of this endangered species exist in the world. In the wild, Asiatic lions are found only in the Gir Forest of India.

Above: Despite his size and fierce reputation, this male Asian lion (Panthera leo persica) *spends up to 20 hours a day resting or sleeping.*

Top right: The Grevy's zebra (Equus grevyi), *the largest member of the wild horse family, is known for its beautiful narrow stripes and large ears. The species is endangered due to poaching for skins.*

Bottom right: These Siberian ibex (Capra ibex sibirica) *are right at home on the rugged, rocky crags of the Park's Mountain Habitat. Infant ibex are up and running on these cliffs within minutes after birth.*

Asian Lions

Across the monorail tracks from the Sumatran tigers, but higher up in the same brush-covered valley, are three prides of endangered Asian lions, whose prolific breeding efforts have actually necessitated a temporary birth-control program. This anomaly in the zoo world, for a species that numbers barely 200 in the wild — all in a 500-square-mile sanctuary in the Gir Forest of India — reflects efforts to maintain proper captive breeding within the Species Survival Plan.

Lions, like most cats, breed easily in captivity, once compatible prides are established. So the challenge is to control and manage the rate of reproduction by specific animals, especially in a species such as the Asian lion, where just 150 animals exist in captivity. Participating zoos circulate their animals to facilitate genetic matchups that will minimize the threat of inbreeding, thereby keeping the captive population healthy and productive for generations to come.

Complicating and even stalling the propagation effort of the Asian lion — an endangered species less prolific than the African lion — is the fact that relatively few zoos house Asian lions, thus leaving no market for excess offspring. "If zoos have the facilities to house large cats, most of

them already have African lions — an animal you can easily replace for $50 — and they don't have extra display room for Asian lions," explained Jim Dolan. "Since Asians are much more in need of attention, we're advocating that when zoos need lions in the future, they should seek out Asians through the SSP coordinator, whose job is to recommend preferred generic pairings from among the lions being housed at six participating institutions."

The Wild Animal Park began its Asian lion breeding program in 1981. Once keepers managed to integrate 13 adult lions into three harmonious prides, a population explosion hit, and 12 cubs were born in a year's time. When it became evident that a limited market existed for these offspring, the Park's adult females were surgically implanted with a progesterone contraceptive. "When more zoos and facilities are available to house Asian lions, we'll get back into breeding," said Dolan. "It's a simple process to surgically remove the implant, and it does no harm to the cat."

One way in which the Wild Animal Park managed to reduce its large population was by donating four cubs to the Holy Land Conservation Fund to establish a breeding group at the Hai Bar South Reserve in the Negev Desert of Israel.

Grevy's Zebras

Past the lions and north of Eastern Africa is the densely vegetated home for Grevy's zebras. The Wild Animal Park has had more than 80 births of this endangered species.

Mountain Habitat

This steep, rocky hillside across from the Asian Waterhole provides an eight-acre naturalistic terrain for two goat species, the Siberian ibex and the Himalayan tahr.

Mongolian Steppe

Along the eastern side of the Southern Africa exhibit, the monorail passes a three-acre hillside enclosure containing a large herd of Przewalski's wild horses and a Bactrian (two-hump) camel.

Conservation efforts on behalf of the Przewalski's horse represent a heartening example of how international cooperation can save a species from extinction while helping to safeguard its genetic future. This species, in fact, is the last never-domesticated wild horse left in the world, descendants of the horses depicted in ancient cave paintings at Lascaux, France. They haven't been seen in their native central Asian habitat since 1968.

Currently, about 500 Przewalski's horses reside in 75 zoos and private collections around the world, and it is Oliver Ryder's job, as coordinator for the Species Survival Plan, to make breeding decisions for the entire herd. Ryder, the Zoological Society's geneticist, compiled a complete genealogy of the captive population, which dates back 11 generations; he now uses a computer to determine how closely two potential mates are related, and, hence, the advisability of such a union. Retaining genetic variability is critical, for there are indications that inbreeding already has shortened the horses' life spans and their period of sexual maturity to the point where successful mating is increasingly difficult.

To counteract this development, Ryder and others on the SSP committee have worked across political boundaries

International breeding loans have helped save the Przewalski's wild horse (Equus p. przewalskii) from extinction. This species is the progenitor of all domestic horses.

to arrange breeding loans that will improve the gene pool of the overall population. For instance, in 1981, three mares from the Wild Animal Park herd were flown to the Prague Zoo, halfway around the world, to rendezvous with a prized stallion, Bars, whose mother, Orlitza III, was wild-caught in 1947.

A year later, after two years of negotiations and clearance through diplomatic channels, San Diego arranged a six-horse swap with the Soviet Union — three horses from the U.S. in exchange for two mares and a stallion, who represented unrelated blood in this country. This type of juggling continues, with certain stallions moving from one zoo to another to introduce their bloodlines. Eventually, a selected herd may be released into the wild.

Baboon Hill

As the monorail passes the large pond at the lower end of Eastern Africa, visitors come upon Baboon Hill, a two-acre enclosure for about 12 mandrills, the most endangered members of the baboon family. This grassy exhibit contains date palm trees and a shallow pool, and plans are proceeding to add a recirculating stream (mandrills enjoy water).

East African Bongo and Okapi

Just past Baboon Hill, along the monorail, are large adjoining exhibits — wooded and grassy

— for two of the Wild Animal Park's rarest species, the East African bongo and the okapi.

Large beautifully marked forest antelopes, bongos are rarely seen in the wild or in captivity. Their enclosure was completed in 1984, in hopes of enhancing a thriving breeding group. Four females were born in the following year, and part of this group will be shipped to China in ongoing animal transactions with that country's zoos.

The uniquely colored okapi resemble zebras, but are forest-living relatives of the giraffe. Shy and elusive, they are native to the humid forests of Zaire, where their export is prohibited. About 60 okapi live in zoos around the world, including just three breeding groups in North America — at the Wild Animal Park, Brookfield Zoo in Chicago,

and the Dallas Zoo. Thus, considerable inter-zoo cooperation is needed to continue the species in North America, which has a much smaller population of animals than does Europe.

"Trading and exchanging okapi is a slow process," explained Rich Massena, mammal manager at the Park. "Not that many people have them, and they're such a delicate, expensive animal that people want to cover all their bases before they move these animals. Yet we all know that we have to ship animals around to make the best use of the available blood stock." Since nobody knows how many okapi exist in the wild, and exporting them from Zaire is virtually impossible, captive breeding programs may be their only chance for survival.

Left: The mandrill (Mandrillus sphinx), native to the rain forests of equatorial Africa, is one of several endangered primate species at the Wild Animal Park.

Right: The East African bongo (Tragelaphus eurycerus issaaci) is one of the rarest and least well-known antelopes. Though their striped coats look conspicuous in the open, they are well-camouflaged in their native dense forests of central Africa.

In Nairobi Village

Western Lowland Gorillas

In the wilds of Africa, habitat destruction and poaching have so reduced the lowland and mountain gorillas that one observer has described them as "an international treasure on the edge of extinction." Recognizing this plight years ago, San Diego Wild Animal Park personnel have devoted painstaking efforts to establish and maintain a successful troop of lowland gorillas.

Trib has been the troop's patriarch since 1972, when he was moved to the Park from the San Diego Zoo. Having arrived there 12 years earlier as a wild-born, orphaned youngster, he has made a significant contribution to the gorilla's captive population by siring five offspring, including two youngsters born to females who honeymooned at the Park and gave birth elsewhere.

Trib's peaceful family unit was expanded in May 1984 when the Zoological Society received a gift of four adult gorillas from a private primate collection in England: a female, Katie, and three males, Ollie, Winston, and Tsambo. In the hope that the new animals would strengthen the Wild Animal Park's breeding program, a long, slow process began to integrate the gorillas into two breeding groups.

The gorillas occupy a grassy, landscaped knoll, on view near the end of the monorail tour. When not on exhibit, they live in a large bedroom area, measuring more than 1,500 square feet, which contains separate sleeping quarters. The residents are usually sound asleep, lying on their backs or on their sides, when the keeper arrives between 6:00 and 6:30 a.m. "I first give them some solid food to work on — apples, oranges, bananas, carrots, onions, lettuce, and monkey chow biscuits — while I make up their bottles," said Peggy Sexton, who shares keeper duties with Sue Doleshal. The 32-ounce bottles contain evaporated milk diluted with water and a spoonful of vitamin syrup.

After that, the keeper cleans the outside exhibit, hosing off the grass and raking up debris from the day before. Then she lets one group of gorillas into the exhibit area before the Park opens. Back inside, she cleans the bedroom areas and gives the gorillas a fresh supply of hay. "Some of them fashion a bed from the hay," said Sexton, "and some don't care, but they all like to eat it or play with it. The hay gives them something to do and is a good stimulus."

Out on exhibit, two of the young gorillas, Alberta and Jitu, are the public's favorites. "Everybody likes them because they're such characters," said Peggy Sexton. "They were both hand-raised as babies and are used to being around people, but a lot of their clowning around is due to age — even in the wild, young gorillas are really playful."

Alberta and Jitu clap their hands and make different noises, trying to get people's attention, and sometimes do somersaults. "They interact with the public," said Sexton, "but they also play a lot together and they really get into it; they wrestle and chase each other and play-bite. Trib prefers to just sit there and let them attack him. They come charging at him and he'll swat at them, and make faces, and vocalize, but you can tell he's having fun, that it's not antagonistic behavior."

Ring-Tailed Lemurs

A frisky band of ring-tailed lemurs entertains visitors in Nairobi Village, swinging and leaping through the leafy branches of three large rubber trees on their grassy island enclosure. These beautiful and gentle primates, distinguished by their large eyes, foxlike muzzles, thick fur coats, and long bushy tails, also represent a species that may escape extinction only through captive breeding efforts.

Eons ago, when a cataclysmic geologic rift separated the island of Madagascar from the mainland of Africa,

the lemur began to evolve into an astounding variety of species on this "island that time forgot." But eventually man arrived. Today, Madagascar's once-vast rain forest has been largely destroyed, and the remaining forests are fast disappearing, eliminating the lemur's natural habitat. While numerous natural preserves exist, hunting in the wild is virtually unchecked; and, at present, the Malagasy government does not allow exportation of lemurs.

Twenty lemur species survive, but only eight are found in zoos. Of these eight, the Zoological Society of San Diego has four: ring-tailed, red ruffed, black-and-white ruffed, and black. Thus, the lemur's plight has become a special project of the research department.

"Lemurs breed fairly well," noted trustee Dr. Kurt Benirschke, "but there are problems we need to solve — like why some animals breed and others do not, and why there are incompatible pairs." So studies are underway on lemur reproductive cycles, genetics, behavior, and nutrition, with artificial insemination seen as a future alternative in the effort to perpetuate lemur species in captivity — no matter what happens in Madagascar.

Hanuman Langurs

S agar Tal, the landscaped home for the Hanuman langurs, is one of the most accessible exhibits at the Wild Animal Park, allowing visitors to view them at a close range and from several levels. Hanuman langurs are considered sacred in India, where they are associated with the Hindu god Hanuman, but are still endangered there because human overcrowding is reducing the amount of suitable habitat.

The Wild Animal Park's group of Hanuman langurs has produced 18 offspring while in residence. "People like the Hanumans because they can get close and observe a lot of interaction as the animals eat and play," said keeper Peggy Sexton.

Golden Lion Tamarins

These small orange primates live in glass-front enclosures that have painted naturalistic backgrounds, live plants, and filtered sunlight in the Animal Care Center. Two pairs arrived at the Wild Animal Park in 1984, and represent an effort by the Zoological Society to concentrate more on certain South American primates that are difficult to manage in captivity.

Tamarins are larger than their cousins, the marmosets, and have been rescued from almost certain extinction by conservation efforts, notably those of the Los Angeles Zoo, National Zoo, and Jersey Wildlife Trust.

Queensland Koalas

Another featured species living at the Animal Care Center is a small group of koalas, a marsupial (not a bear) native to Australia. They were moved to the Wild Animal Park in 1983 after a population explosion boosted the San Diego Zoo's koala colony to nearly 20 individuals.

The koala — with its fur-fringed ears, shoe-button eyes, and quizzical expression — is one of the world's most popular animals. At the Park, a glass-fronted enclosure allows visitors a close-up view of the marsupials as they move about in their perching trees, doze away the hours, or munch on their sole food supply — eucalyptus leaves and tender stems, as well as seed pods and flowers at certain times of year.

When the koalas first arrived at the Wild Animal Park, they were displayed in an outside exhibit with eucalyptus trees for climbing. That proved too tempting for escapes, so they were moved inside permanently. Long-range plans, however, still include a walk-through koala exhibit with a large breeding colony. For now, the founding residents include Euc, a wild-born male that arrived at the Zoo in 1981, and three breeding-age females, Adelle, Fifi, and Peg. Euc has his own quarters, while the females each have a tree, with a pole between their stalls that allows them to visit back and forth. As they come into estrus, they are paired with Euc for breeding.

Kirk's Dik-Diks

Scattered throughout Nairobi Village are a number of small, carefully landscaped exhibits for animals such as spider monkeys, suni antelopes, slender-horned gazelles, and Kirk's dik-diks, one of the smallest species of antelope, which stand only 12 to 15 inches at the shoulder when full-grown.

Two new exhibits were designed for the dik-diks that closely resemble the desert thorn scrub of their native African habitat. Sand creates a desert terrain; and each exhibit has been planted with patches of aloe, acacia scrub, and feather grass. "Dik-diks are extremely shy and elusive, and they need hiding areas like this," noted Nairobi Village keeper Linda Thompson. "We hope our animals will feel at home in these enclosures and successfully reproduce."

Exotic Waterfowl Lagoons

Along the banks of the main lagoon in Nairobi Village, visitors can enjoy a variety of aquatic plants and domestic and exotic fowl — from black swans found only in Western Australia to old-world comb ducks found only in Africa, and coscoroba swans, native to South America.

To encourage reproduction by the Chilean flamingos, their Nairobi Village home was extensively modified and expanded in 1984. The grassy area was tripled, and a nesting place was established that included a pond, a series of "bubblers," and a system of misters hidden among the bird of paradise plants surrounding the pond. Until 1983, when the Wild Animal Park's colony of 18 flamingos was augmented by 18 birds obtained from the wild, the flock was too small for breeding. Experience shows that at least 10 pairs of birds are required to initiate breeding behavior.

Above: Considered by many to be the most beautiful of African waterfowl, the pygmy goose (Nettapus auritus) *is actually a duck, but was named a goose because of the shape of its bill.*

Right: The Congo River Fishing Bridge provides a dramatic backdrop for these Chilean flamingos (Phoenicopterus chilensis). *Two large flocks of African flamingos live in the Park's expansive African exhibits.*

Animal Care Center

This bustling complex, staffed by about 10 keepers, is an important focal point at the Wild Animal Park, both in terms of animal care, and public education and enjoyment. All the diets for birds living in Nairobi Village are prepared here, while other keepers attend to a variety of ailing or orphaned young animals brought in from around the Park for hand-raising — until they are old enough to be reintroduced into an exhibit or shipped to another zoo. Meanwhile, windows allow visitors to watch food preparation and the care of infant animals, and a Petting Kraal affords a chance to mingle with various exotic animals.

Over the years, a marvelous variety of newborns have been hand-raised at the Animal Care Center, including a white rhino, a giraffe, a water buffalo, gorillas, a tiger, lions, a cheetah, zebras, a pygmy hippo, hornbills, and numerous antelopes and deer. Some babies were brought in for obvious life-and-death reasons; they've been injured, they're sick, or they've been rejected or neglected by their mothers. "Also," said Terry Blakeslee, lead keeper of the Animal Care Center, "if an animal is destined to be shipped to another zoo, it's easier on the animal to be captured as a newborn and hand-raised than to be caught as an adult. When a baby is brought in the minute it's born, it's healthy, it hasn't had time to suffer an injury, and it hasn't nursed from its mother, so it doesn't realize the difference with our bottles. But if a baby has nursed from its mom, we usually have to resort to all kinds of tricks to get it to take a bottle."

One of the keepers' favorite animals to pass through the Care Center in recent years was Helen, the pygmy hippo, born in the Eastern Africa exhibit.

Top: The petting Kraal in Nairobi Village allows visitors to mingle with and feed many hand-raised exotic species.

Bottom: Small in stature but not in threats, this pygmy hippopotamus (Choeropsis liberiensis) snarls at keepers as they approach its island in the Eastern Africa enclosure.

Above left: More than a dozen rare bird species, like these tarictic hornbills (Penelopides panini manillae) from the Philippines, are kept off public exhibit to maximize their breeding potential.

Above right: The marabou stork (Leptoptilos crumeniferus) has often been called the world's ugliest bird.

Top right: The white-backed vulture (Gyps africanus) is one of many species of large African birds at the Park.

Top far right: A living example of nature's artistry, these vulturine guineafowl (Acryllium vulturinum) display a palette of iridescent plumage in their Nairobi Village home.

Bottom right: The first exhibit is the entrance aviary, where more than 100 tropical African birds fly freely in a dense jungle habitat.

Earlier, two hippo newborns were left in the exhibit to be raised by the parents, and both died from neglect. This time, keepers brought Helen in the moment she was born, as the mother was unwilling to take care of her. Helen had no health problems to overcome, and she started nursing from a bottle almost immediately. Over the next six months, she gained almost a pound a day.

Helen's introduction into the Petting Kraal, which adjoins the Animal Care Center, was a surprise for the "regulars" — various sheep and goats — although she never gave them any cause for being afraid.

"She would just toddle around the enclosure, slowly ambling wherever her nose led her," recalled Terry Blakeslee, "and I think she would have played with the other animals, but they were all afraid of her — this strange-looking new creature without fur. When we first put her out in the Kraal every morning, the sheep, goats, and deer would all run to the other end. Usually they're all inter-mingled, but when there's something new out there that alarms them, each

species bands together. Even after four months, they would still keep their distance. We had the same type of reaction from the animals when we used to raise white rhinos."

As Blakeslee talked, she watched Helen drink from a plastic water tub in the hot morning sun. Moments later, the little hippo fell asleep with her head resting on the edge of the tub. "Helen has been sold to another zoo," she said wistfully, "but I'm trying to hide her."

Hornbills are another favorite of the keepers. "They all seem to be characters," said Blakeslee. "They like to get up on the sheep when the sheep are sitting down, but then jump off when they get up. One hornbill, though, liked to stay on for a ride."

Then there was Kukawia, the young Abyssinian ground hornbill, who would preen the antelopes, pull tails, try to untie people's shoelaces, or chase things — like kids running away from her. But when she plucked a pearl from a visitor's ring and swallowed it, she had to be removed to an area with less public contact.

The California Native Plants Trail offers visitors a chance to get close to many rare specimens. Ten major botanical communities, from the deserts to the High Sierras, are represented. Inset: Pincushion proteas (Leucospermum nutans) are one of hundreds of exotic African plants that have been imported for landscaping the Wild Animal Park. More than a dozen special gardens in Nairobi Village and on the Kilimanjaro Trail highlight the Park's unusual collection.

Botanical Collection

Just as the Wild Animal Park's animal collection continues to achieve successes, the horticulture department is creating a botanical haven where the preservation and propagation of endangered flora is a major concern. Starting from its scrub-brush beginnings, the Park has matured and expanded into a botanical garden that requires maintenance of more than 1.5 million plants and trees. A recent computer update showed 2,560 species at the Park, including several hundred endangered plants.

For instance, the Wild Animal Park has been successful cultivating aloes, which are rapidly disappearing from their native habitat in South Africa, cycads (palmlike trees with fernlike leaves), euphorbias, tree ferns, proteas, and cacti. New species of endangered

plants are added each year.

Trails and specialized gardens throughout the Wild Animal Park provide the novice plant enthusiast, as well as the seasoned botanist, with opportunities to study a large number of plants otherwise seen and studied only through much travel and often at great expense. For example, there's the Native Plants Trail leading off the Kilimanjaro Trail by the suspension bridge, and new areas for palms, proteas, herbs, and plants native to Baja California.

Two new gardens have opened in the Park's nursery area — a shade structure filled with epiphyllums and a fuchsia shade house serving as a demonstration garden, with more than 2,000 plants hanging in pots and exhibited in ground displays. The Fuchsia Garden also displays other shade-loving plants and includes a 15-foot waterfall.

The Wild Animal Park's extensive

nursery program grows many of the trees planted in the field exhibits. "We try to match the tree with the animal," said Jim Gibbons, chief horticulturist. "In the Asian exhibits, we use the varieties of *Ficus* and mulberry which come from Asia. In the African areas, we've planted thorn acacias that we've grown from seed. We also use California peppers, which grow similar to other trees from arid parts of southern Africa. Also coral trees and *Podocarpus.* There aren't many things from the swampy wetlands of Asia that will grow in the Asian Waterhole, so we use Australian *Ficus,* which gives the landscape a similar look."

Another ongoing challenge for the horticulture department is keeping the animals from eating or uprooting shade trees planted in the main compounds. A rhino, for instance, may not be able to reach the lowest branches of a young tree, nor even wish to snack, but it does like to rub its horn and hide, and can easily push the tree out of the ground.

"At first," said Gibbons, "we simply placed sharp rocks around the trees to keep the rhinos out, since they have tender feet. But then we noticed that animals like the buffalo and antelope would carefully tiptoe through the rocks and take out a tree by nibbling the bark. So we had to start protecting trees by wrapping them loosely with chain link."

The goal is to get the tree's lowest branches above or away from the tallest animal in an exhibit — a major task in Eastern Africa, which is home to the Ugandan giraffe. Here, vulnerable trees are protected by log stockades or a ring of rocks, but keepers must constantly monitor activity. Giraffes are persistent, and if the soil around a protective barrier builds up two or three inches from erosion runoff, putting the branches within their reach, they will begin to nibble the tree. Said Gibbons, "You can lose a big tree within two nights if you're not careful."

The horticulture department also maintains a 14-acre browse farm planted with thousands of eucalyptus and acacias. The trees are harvested daily to feed the koalas and to supplement the diets of many Wild Animal Park animals.

The kaffirboom coral tree (Erythrina caffra) *is among dozens of spectacular blooming trees from Africa that are planted throughout the Wild Animal Park.*

Your Visit to the San Diego Wild Animal Park

The San Diego Wild Animal Park opened in May 1972 as a haven for the world's vanishing wildlife species. It is comprised of a 17-acre African village — Nairobi Village — in which small mammals and birds are exhibited, and restaurants, gift shops, and visitor convenience facilities are located. The rest of the Park's 700 developed acres are visible only from the Wgasa Bush Line monorail that travels the five-mile perimeter of Asian and African animal habitats and the Kilimanjaro Trail.

The Wild Animal Park is a private, non-profit enterprise dedicated to saving the world's rare and endangered plant and animal wildlife, and depends on monetary support through ticket sales, food and gift purchases, and membership support. Donations are also gladly accepted.

We thank you for your support and hope you have a memorable day at the San Diego Wild Animal Park.

Above: Only 700 of the Park's 1,800 acres have been developed. Most of the 2,200 animals live in expansive (more than 75 acres) enclosures modeled after their native African and Asian habitats.

Previous page left: In summer, Nairobi Village bustles with evening entertainment, and nighttime monorail tours offer an unparalleled look at the animals' nocturnal behaviors. Right: Visitors encounter their first glimpse of Africa on California Highway 78 at the entrance to the Wild Animal Park.

ANIMAL EXHIBITS
(E=endangered species)

Entrance Aviary: Your first look at the Wild Animal Park is one of the world's largest suspension flight aviaries, containing scores of birds from Africa amid dense vegetation, a waterfall, and ponds.

DeBrazza's guenons: Stop to admire these old-world monkeys as they leap about in their enclosure.

Spider monkeys: Perhaps the greatest comics at the Wild Animal Park, these acrobats can entertain while you dine at Thorn Tree Terrace.

Zulu suni and dik-diks: See these miniatures of the antelope family in exhibits that replicate their homelands.

Waterfowl lagoon: Hundreds of ducks call Nairobi Lagoon home. Some belong to the Wild Animal Park, but many are free-loaders. Look for the exhibits for Chilean flamingos and black swans.

Lemur Isle (E): Once you see these cuddly primates, you'll know why many people confuse them with cats or raccoons.

Slender-horned gazelles (E): One of the rarest gazelles in the world lives and breeds at the Wild Animal Park.

Petting Kraal: The young and young-at-heart enjoy petting exotic sheep, goats, deer, and antelopes here. Some of the goats eat anything, so please keep all paper products out of sight.

Animal Care Center (E): Here you can see small mammals that need specialized care and exhibits such as koalas and golden lion tamarins. You can also watch as keepers prepare food for all the animals in Nairobi Village. The Animal Care Center is home to many sick or orphaned youngsters whose mothers couldn't care for them.

Tropical America: Step into the tropics where squirrel monkeys, small deer, and hundreds of birds are free-roaming with the visitors. This walk-through exhibit features plants and animals from Central and South America.

Hanuman langurs (E): Stroll on the elevated bridge to the treetops where rare black-faced monkeys of India frolic. Small muntjac deer live with the monkeys.

Gorilla Grotto (E): See our large colony of gorillas. Watch for Trib, Dolly, Katie, Vila, Alberta, Jitu, and Winston as they play in their expansive grassy grotto.

THE KILIMANJARO TRAIL

Take all or part of this 1.25-mile trail to see some of the Wild Animal Park's larger inhabitants and many special gardens.

Australian Rain Forest: One of the newest features of the Wild Animal Park shows off hundreds of exotic South Pacific plant, bird, and mammal species. It actually mist-rains in the forest several times each day. Here you can see exquisite rainbow lorikeets, rose-breasted cockatoos, wallabies, kangaroos, emus, and more.

Cheetahs (E): Meet the world's fastest land mammal on the Trail. Look closely for these spotted cats — they hide in the tall grass.

Sumatran tigers (E): One of the most majestic of all cats, the Sumatran tiger is also very elusive. Early morning or late afternoon is when they're most active.

Asian lions (E): Though hard to distinguish from their African cousins, these Asian lions are highly endangered and rarely seen in zoological collections. Come see our pride.

Nyala exhibit: See these large and striking antelopes near the African elephants, with East African crowned cranes.

Above: The Park is colorful year-round. In fall, these Chinese pistachio (Pistacia chinensis) trees on the Kilimanjaro Trail are particularly vibrant.

Left: The Wild Animal Park has the world's largest collection of hooved animals with over 90 species represented. The Armenian mouflon (Ovis orientalis gmelini) is one of several sheep species exhibited.

61

Above: Africa-styled Mombasa Cooker and other restaurants and gift shops in Nairobi Village have something for every visitor's taste.

Right: Male Ugandan giraffes (Giraffa camelopardalis rothschildi)) sparring for dominance is a behavior rarely seen in other zoos. The Wild Animal Park's similarity to animals' native habitats encourages displays of natural behavior.

Pumzika Point: From the lookout platform, you can see most of the 125-acre Eastern Africa enclosure. Among the species you'll see are Uganda giraffe, white-bearded gnu, Patterson's eland, Cape buffalo, Kenya impala, and a very rare rhinoceros. You might even see a flock of flamingos or a pair of pygmy hippopotomuses in the Eastern Africa lake.

GARDENS ON THE TRAIL

Before you head onto the Trail, ask about the availability of a guide to show you the unusual horticulture collection.

Herb Garden: Near the African elephants.

California Native Plants Trail: In bloom throughout spring, located near the suspension bridge.

Protea Garden: Across from the lion bedrooms.

Conifer Arboretum: Hundreds of species of conifers from around the world.

Epiphyllum House: Up the Trail from the African elephant barn. More than 150 plants; most bloom in May.

Fuchsia Garden: In bloom throughout the year. Adjacent to the Epiphyllum House.

GIFT SHOPS

The Bazaar: Take home a piece of Africa with rare African artifacts and cultural trinkets from around the world. Also T-shirts, designer clothes, hats, accessories, jewelry, china, pottery, books, posters, and a children's department with toys to suit every taste.

The T-Shirt Shop: Designer and custom T-shirts for everyone in the family. Also hats and sunglasses.

The Plant Trader: Take home something live! The Plant Trader is full of landscaping and house plants — from exotic to easy-to-grow varieties. The staff will give you pointers on how to keep your plant healthy.

The Camera Hut: Here you can borrow a camera with a film purchase, rent binoculars, and find all the photography supplies to make your Wild Animal Park visit memorable. Even postcards and a mailbox to write home to family and friends.

Natural barriers and moats enable visitors and animals to be just feet apart in Nairobi Village. Here visitors examine Chilean flamingos (Phoenicopterus chilensis) up close near the Park's entrance.

FOOD SERVICE

Congo Kitchen: Breakfast, sandwiches, coffee, lunch, and ice-cream treats.

Thorn Tree Terrace: Cafeteria-style buffet with hamburgers, sandwiches, and chicken platters.

Kafferboom Cupboard: Across from the Petting Kraal. Features delicious sandwiches and dessert specialties.

Mombasa Cooker: Overlooking Nairobi Lagoon. Features hamburgers, chicken sandwiches, fries, dinner platters, beer, wine, and soft drinks.

Super Safari Cones: A special indulgence of rich ice cream in a waffle cone smothered in your choice of sundae topping, whipped cream, and nuts.

Samburu Barbecue Terrace: Overlooking the green San Pasqual Valley and Eastern Africa. Barbecued beef sandwiches and dinners, chicken platters, fries, zucchini, cakes, and pastries.

Other foodstands are located throughout Nairobi Village to serve you with beverages, snacks, and desserts.

Picnic facilities: Picnic tables are located across from the Elephant Wash and on the Kilimanjaro Trail near Pumzika Point and the Savannah.

Mombasa Pavilion: Overlooking the lagoon. Available for private parties. Contact Group Sales for more information.

VISITOR SERVICES

First Aid: Please report any injuries to the First Aid Office in the Administration Building.

Information: Feel free to ask any employee, or stop by Visitor Services in the entry area or the Administration Building.

Strollers and Wheelchairs: Rented on a first-come, first-served basis near the Camera Hut at the entrance.

Visitor Services: Zoological Society membership renewals or purchases, Photo Caravan reservations, and group tour information.

ANIMAL SHOWS

Bird Show: You're guaranteed to laugh at funny parrots, yet marvel at the beauty of an eagle, and be awestruck on the plight of many endangered birds in this unique presentation of free-flight birds.

Elephant Show: Witness the amazing natural behaviors of Asian elephants, and learn how they've worked with man for thousands of years.

Animal Antics: See both common and unusual domestic birds, dogs, and cats exhibit amazing natural behaviors.

Critter Encounter: Our trainers bring out exotic animals to meet visitors up close. Meet a cheetah, kinkajou, addax, snakes, and birds.